SECURE YOUR OWN MASK

Secure Your Own Mask

Shaindel Beers

Charlotte —
I hope these poems find
a home in your heart!
♡, Shaindel
10/15/22
Pendleton, OR

WHITE PINE PRESS / BUFFALO. NEW YORK

WHITE PINE PRESS
P.O. Box 236
Buffalo, NY 14201
www.whitepine.org

Acknowledgments:
Grateful acknowledgment is made to the following journals in which these poems, some of them in earlier versions (or in parts), first appeared:

Barn Owl Review (online), reprinted in *VoiceIn Journal* and *Red Sky: Poetry on the Global Epidemic of Violence Against Women*: "The (Im)Precision of Language.
Thank You For Swallowing: "Secure Your Mask Before Helping Others" and
        "Playing Dolls."
The Nervous Breakdown: "When we were knife throwers."
The Rumpus:"One Gaza Family Observes a Grim Holiday in Wartime."
        (Acknowledgments continue on page 105.)

Publication of this book was made possible, in part, by public funds from the New York State Council on the Arts, a State Agency.

Cover Art by Heldáy de la Cruz.

Printed and bound in the United States of America.

Library of Congress Control Number: 2017956278

ISBN 978-1-945680-17-5

My thanks to Blue Mountain Community College for financing my trips to writers' conferences and workshops to further this work. Thank you to the faculty at Quest Writer's Conference, especially to Gregory Orr who helped me shape the title poem for this collection and to Joy Harjo, who has been an influence since we met nearly twenty years ago. Thank you especially to Ki Russell for her continued friendship and keen editing skills.

Many thanks to Jenn Givhan for her guidance in editing this manuscript and to Dennis Maloney, Alan Michael Parker, and White Pine Press for selecting this collection as their prize winner. I'm indebted to Maggie Smith, Robert Wrigley, Rhett Miller, and Heldáy de la Cruz for the words and art that grace the covers of this book.

Much gratitude to Robert Lee Brewer for the writing prompts which inspired many of these poems. Thanks also to Jesse Ahmann and Skip vonKuske for collaborating on cross-genre interpretations of these pieces.

Love to Matthew DeGarmo for his kindness and patience in all things and to Liam for letting me write about him, even though it is "so embarrassing."

Contents

III.

IV.

I.

The (Im)Precision of Language

How far the ring-necked dove is
from wringing a dove's neck. The way
a stand of trees can hide a deer

stand, concealing the hunter who
will shoot the deer. The deer, who will
fall in the fall in the fallow field.

Once, someone who was dear to me
threatened me with a deer rifle. Cleaned
it random times, out of season when

he was upset. Said, *I don't want to be
divorced. We can make this work,* while
working the polishing cloth along the metal

barrel of the gun. My blood barreled through
my body when I would see his truck in the drive.
I was never not scared to come home, to fall

asleep, to say the least little thing wrong.
Language became a tricky game where saying
nothing meant everything, where saying everything

meant nothing left to fear. I sang my sorrow
to anyone who recognized the panic
of birdsong, the desperation of the killdeer

feigning its broken wing. Anything to lure the predator
from its nest. Its broken wing
was strength. I shone my brokenness

like a flare gun. Someone might understand the bird
of my heart always crashing against the cage
of my ribs, the moth of hidden fear fluttering

to escape from my throat. Once, in my Shakespeare
class I learned that *brace* meant a pair, a brace
of kinsmen, of harlots, of greyhounds,

a brace of warlike brothers. In another time
I stood at the front of the classroom in a chest
brace because my husband had collapsed

the cartilage between my ribs. I couldn't reach
the string on the movie screen and had to ask
for help. I said, *I'm wearing a brace, so I can't*

stretch. I thought of the grimace stretching
across the nurse's face when I said, *I know,*
this sounds like domestic violence. It was an accident,

just goofing around. I wrapped the Velcro belt
around my ribs each morning as he ribbed me
I should've given up, what was I trying to prove

staying in a submission hold
until he cracked my ribs? Was I
stupid? Or just stubborn? I didn't know

he was grooming me for greater violence,
the rock thrown at me in the car,
the wedding ring pressed so tight

by his hand holding mine until I bled.
Which brings us back to the dove,
the difference between ringing

and wringing and where language leaves us
when someone controls every word we say,
when we have no one left to talk to.

Secure Your Mask Before Helping Others

I.

Because soon you won't have any needs of your own.
They will all be for him. You will be walking to the middle
of the lake, your pockets filled with all the prettiest stones.

Amethyst, quartz, peridot. All the beauty it could ever take
to drown you. The topaz and emerald of the water.
The sapphire and ruby of police lights.

Until you are as beaded as a twenty-pound wedding gown.
And aren't you beautiful? You are the prettiest girl
at the Harvest Moon Ball. Why aren't you grateful?

No one has ever been so adorned with abjection.
There are so many women in line for him, each one
a corpse bride in waiting. Any girl would treasure

the feel of his boot on her throat, to pay off the court fines,
to hide him from the police, to say that they were your painkillers.

II.

You wanted to know what it was like to have pearls
on the inside. To wash down five, six, seven—

all good girls go to Heaven—Percocet
with the amber of whiskey. And he knew you would do it—
your drinking was always the problem. He knew it the first time

he saw you. Imagine if you would have tried heroin.

Boy, could he tell you stories.
Graduate school doesn't sound that different from rehab;

don't feel so special. You would be in the same place
no matter where you started out.

III.

Girls like you are so easy
to manipulate. Because the bruise is already there,

he just has to press. Other names have already been scalpeled
into your skin. Look how you bleed these pomegranate drops.
Why aren't you crying?

What's wrong with you?
Have you gone dumb? Or numb?

IV.

This is like being married to a fucking baby.
You would probably kill a baby.
You're the abusive one. You're the one with anger issues.

No, what we should do is have a baby.
That will make everything better.
You and me in one person.
I don't know why I didn't think of it before.

We'll name her Pearl. We'll cast her before swine.
She will be our savior. You don't really believe
any of this shit, do you? It's just a game,

but there's no scoring system. Lean down so I can place
the medals around your neck. The medals
will weigh you down until I win—

gold and silver and bronze, and don't take any wooden
nickels though you're lucky I give you anything,
you worthless bitch.

Oh, look, here's the oxygen mask.
Here's your chance to save me.
Put it over my face and let me breathe.

The Mechatronic Bird
Falls in Love with the Real and Vice Versa

Once the bird in the cuckoo clock spied his beloved.
Ruby-throated and emerald winged, flitting outside
the window. Ethereal. Unreal. When he was only wood-
grain and gear and cog. Tiny hammer ticking out time.
Would she ever be there when he was next allowed
to sing out a new hour? What would it be like to sip
agave, Karo syrup, any sweet thing from a flower,
real or man-made? If he can just make it to the window,
maybe she'll tell him her secrets.

The peregrine falcon eyes the plastic owl. His stoic
stare. The shriek that echoes from speakers in the back
of his head. The peregrine knows that the pigeons
scatter when the animatronic owl shrieks, while he
has to dive 200 mph in pursuit of his prey. He longs
for the owl's power. That patience. How does the owl
do what he does, sun after moon after sun? Doesn't
he ever long to fly home to be with other owls?

The decoy duck is pulled out of the burlap bag. Placed
in the reeds. He bobs at river's edge, momentarily bathed
in dawnlight. He wants to warn the approaching female,
Don't come close. My kind of beauty is no good for you.
My teal head, russet chest. This is the type of beauty
that kills. What I wouldn't give to touch the purple
iridescent feathers of your underwing. But it is always too late.
There is the bark and the splash. Rustle of wings, report
of gunfire. And then she is gone, into the dog's mouth, no more
alive than he. It is a terrible job being a tiny hollow god
of destruction. What kind of creator crafted him for this?

When we were knife throwers

My favorite part of the act wasn't the sparkle of red sequins,
the skimming of satin skirt flirting with thigh. I loved

the knife *thwack*, the shudder of pearl handle vibrating
when the blade landed true. I loved cartwheeling in space

when you spun the wheel, our love every day a game
of roulette, praying to always land on black but wearing

red just in case. I lived for you tying the blindfold, the whisper,
I love you as you fastened the manacles secure. Each second

a precarious balance between trust and chance.

One Gaza Family Observes a Grim Holiday in Wartime

(after the story of the same title on NPR's *All Things Considered*)

Yesterday my son learned to open the deadbolt.
Upset about his toys forgotten at daycare,
he slipped out the front door while I was changing
clothes, tried to go back to get them himself.
When I came out of the bedroom, he was gone.
For those two minutes, my heart stopped
until I scooped him up crying in the driveway.
Today, I thought of the mothers of Gaza.
We listened to the news while driving to daycare.
One Palestinian child dead every hour. A reporter
was interviewing a family celebrating Eid al-Fitr.
There are 53 people staying in this three-bedroom
apartment, including eight babies. At the sound-clip
of the babies crying, Liam asked, *Baby?*
Are you all right? The reporter is the same one
who interviewed me about my first book, who
helped me dismantle the violence of my childhood.
I want her to be safe, this woman I spent a few hours
with in a radio studio, a few minutes with on the phone,
I want the babies to be safe, their mothers,
their fathers. I don't believe in a god,
neither Christian, nor Jewish, nor
Muslim, but I believe in the peace that can
inhabit a human heart. Meanwhile, in the story,
a four-year-old boy chooses his holiday present,
a toy gun. He delights in the rat-a-tat of the rifle-fire.

Unfriending the Dead

They show up in the Newsfeed. Facebook
as memorial. Birthday reminders. Events where
the guest of honor will never appear. Someone

who has forgotten or who hasn't heard will leave
a joyful, "Eat cake!" a copied and pasted "Happy birthday!"
even just the letters HBD in our light-speed world.

Still not so far away from lost messengers in ancient times,
letters gone down at sea or never delivered because of a lame horse.
But others — "Miss you, Mama. It's been hard."

"This earth isn't the same without you on it." Sometimes
I think about the ways we die. Cancer, car accident,
suicide, suicide, suicide, suicide — I think

of the body hanging. The children unknowing on
the other side of the door while the blood stops travelling,
the cells shut down without oxygen. This is all

very mechanical. It is just lights going out on a cellular
level. The same way pixels spark out of my LED screen
sending their image and are then shut down. Some days

I want to type, "I saw your son in the school concert.
He was wonderful. You would be so proud." Or,
"The earth misses the weight of your terrible beauty."

Is this the modern way of planting flowers in a cemetery?
Placing stones on a grave? Is the digital world temperate
or desert? Victorians must've felt this way about photographs,

and before this, paintings. How are we always inventing
ways to keep the dead with us? Why is it so hard to let
the cursor hover over Unfriend? Block? How permanently

to release you? To make room for more. To keep the pixels
of you from my screen the way the tiny lights of your body
turned out — One, by one, by one.

3.22 Miles

First run through crush of leaves.
Featherlight piles of aspen, yellow litter
of locust. My runner's mantra in time
with my breath — *Breathing in, I calm myself;*
Breathing out, I smile. Calming.
Smiling. The long history of runners without
this luxury. Bare feet that have slipped through sand.
Booted feet skimming or crunching through snow.
In some languages feet are the hands that touch
the ground. The way the potato is the apple
of the earth. The heel strike. The push off
the ball of the foot. The scenery. The grey horse
on the dun hill, which another runner may see
as sniper distance. The truck exhaust, which,
Thank God, isn't the smoke of burning bodies
or villages. The boy I pass at the school bus stop might
in another world be holding a rifle, a machete,
instead of a lunchbox. I have this luxury to utter
mantras. *Slow is the new fast.* To wear out
hundred dollar shoes every 300 miles. To stop
when I want. Slow when I want. Search
for the deer on the ridge with the eyes
of the curious, not the starving.
If I say I am running for my life it is merely
a metaphor about health. A pithy saying
painted on a gym wall. I am lucky.
There is no heart pound of the pursuer
behind me. Just me. Just the foot strikes.
Just breath.

The Secret Rabbit

In the story the woman hits the rabbit on the way home to her husband
from her lover's. *What does the rabbit symbolize?*

Fertility, a student says. *Maybe she wants to get pregnant by
her lover. The death of a new beginning*, says another. *Maybe*

*she can't really leave her husband and just start over. Maybe
the rabbit dying means that she is pregnant like old pregnancy tests*

used to be. Some students look doubtful. They have peed on sticks
that show lines or plus marks, kept the time on smartphones.

The rabbit was white, says another. It is true. In the story,
it was snowing. *No way she could have seen a white rabbit.*

The student continues, *Maybe it's the death of purity.* Other
students like this theory. *But the story doesn't say for sure*

it's a rabbit. She thinks *that she hit a rabbit. It might have been
a cat or a dog. She looks in her rearview mirror and keeps*

driving. It's definitely symbolic of an ending. She can't go back.
What I don't tell them about is my own rabbit. That I had been

drinking. That at 55 mph on a country road, the rabbit panics
and runs straight toward your headlights. I don't tell them

that after this you are just as panicked as the rabbit. Who
can you tell about this? How to explain where you were,

what you were doing driving three beers in at that hour.
Maybe the rabbit saw the light as a rabbit hole. Maybe

it reminded him of first opening his eyes at six days old.
Maybe he saw it as his escape to another world, one free

of coyotes and harsh winters. The way I always saw a man
as an escape hatch to another world because

I was raised to. The way girls were given by their fathers
to a husband to a grave and that was the only story. Until

a man just became an escape hatch to another man,
and all the worlds were eventually the same, this one

with more yelling or less than the previous one, and me
with no way to make a world of my own because I didn't know

how. You keep this rabbit hidden for years from anyone
wondering what it could possibly mean.

The Interview

In the wealthy, suburban Starbucks
with the stone fireplace and parquet floors,
the woman recognizes me from my picture,
pats the chair next to her. We small talk,
size each other up. Out of nowhere, she says,
*I think of young women like you as a present
for my husband.* I picture myself as a gift—
being gifted. I am an object to be unwrapped,
opened, slipped into for a fortieth birthday.
She is stunning. Her hair, the pale yellow
of butter. Eyes, sky blue. I picture Disney
villains—the ones whose only crime is being
replaced, growing old. The wicked queen's
sharp cheekbones. Almond eyes. How she
is more beautiful than Snow White will ever be.
Maleficent, magnificent, with both dragon
and fire inside. The scene where Cinderella's
stepmother's eyes glow green in the dark.
Wolf Woman, something beyond human
that Cinderella someday *might* be. She tells me
about ice climbing. Kicking the crampons
just right into the frozen waterfall. In other lives,
I've loved the creaks and groans of ice breaking,
the heart-stopping *whoosh* of snowslide. She
presses a slip of paper into my palm. She says
it can be *For anything.* I want to be snow princess
aging to ice queen. She is crystalline, blue-veined
at the temples. Fine lines just starting at the eyes.
Is this better than the poisoned apple? Following
the huntsman into the woods? Just different?
We murmur our awkward goodbyes. In the parking lot,
my warming car, I tear her number into flakes,

so I will not call it. Let it dissolve on my tongue.
Imagine her entering my each and every cell.

Self-Portrait as Rosinback Rider

The arch of my foot is perfectly shaped
to withers, to flank. I can stand in arabesque
at a canter. Sweep my back leg through,
backbend, walkover, and land astride.
The hardest part is the smile, the unnatural
strain on the face. It is the difficulty of beauty
pageant smile during athletics. The Paso Fino
beneath me flows like water. His walk
is molasses. I give him molasses mixed
with oats each night. He is sweet as sorghum.
The clop-clop of his hooves is my heartbeat.
Please pray the circus never separates us.
This is the ringmaster's threat when the seats
are empty. A horse costs so much to feed,
and the lions are hungry. This why I cry
into the illustrated man's indigo skin every night.

The Drunk Cowboy Believes in Good

The drunk cowboy has two women cornered at the parking lot party.
The drunk cowboy is solving all of the Mid-East's problems
even though he is drunk and a cowboy and 7,000 miles away

from Israel. He stands tall in his pearl-snap plaid shirt and says,
There's good and evil. And I always side with good. It's like Jesus
and the devil. The women laugh. They offer cogent arguments,

death tolls, ask why it is okay for Israel to fire rockets at schools full
of civilians. *But women and children!,* the women say. *It's like this,*
says the drunk cowboy, *The Israelis told them they could leave.*

It's their own fault for stayin' put. I wonder about the drunk cowboy's
world. He's just a guy at a bar, someone who could have given
George W. Bush acting lessons on how to be the drunk cowboy

President he pretended to be. I want to make it easy for the drunk
cowboy. I want to wear an Evildoer shirt to the band's next gig.
I want to buy Evildoer shirts for the two women debating him.

I want to confuse the drunk cowboy by saying, *See, it's like this.*
There's good and evil. It's like Ahura Mazda and Angra Mainyu.
Teharonhiawako and Tawiskaron, Harry and Voldemort.

A story as old as time. *I'm sure you think I'm stupid,* says the drunk
cowboy. *No, no,* say the women. They are polite. Also, they are women
in the parking lot of a bar at one in the morning. They know

the drunk cowboy is expecting them to soothe his ego, to say
he brought up good points, he's pretty sure in an argument the man
is supposed to win. The women exit, not quite sure what they're escaping.

After *Milkpour #5* by Jessica Plattner

First his cries panicked the horses.
Stall doors kicked down. Fences cleared.
No horses, no plowing. No plowing, no food.
So the men vowed to kill the enormous baby.
No! shrieked the women. *What if he is a god?*
What if the mountains are the breasts
that nourished him? No matter that he was here
in the village far from the mountains.
The women appointed themselves his mothers,
brought bucketfuls of milk from sheep, goats, cows,
hand expressed their own breasts. Made his clothes
from whole fields of cotton and flax.
The enormous baby became the white elephant
who would ruin our village.
Sometimes the path to destruction is saving
the one it takes too much to save.

Perspective

After an image by Hernan Bas

The man stands in the glove shop—
leans his long, thin body, fingers
in soft blue suede, against a railing.
He ponders the discarded glove
on the marble table, which is closest
to us, the viewer. The man is an objet
d'art in the painting. Between us exists
a fourth wall, delicate veil between reality
and illusion. Perhaps the man didn't
exist at all. Maybe there wasn't even
a model. Perhaps he existed only as firings
in the neurons of the artist's brain—
a composite of memory. The eyes of some actor,
the golden hair of an exquisite man who studied
Blake and sat across from him in grad school,
the lips of a smiling barista he saw the morning
the painting was due for his art class.
On the wall next to this imaginary man
is a painting. And how do we know what is real,
what has ever existed in a painting within a painting?
Who is that man? Was there a model? Are we even
in a glove shop because Shakespeare's father was
a glove maker? Are we here because some surnames
denote occupation? Gaunter? Glover?
But what I want to think about is the perspective.
That discarded glove in the foreground. The way
to our eye it is as long as the man's torso and head
put together because it is the object closest to us.
The way that glove may have felt like slipping
into love itself, then was left the way
we thoughtlessly leave things twisted and alone.

How that feeling—its intensity—makes us feel
like the only thing in the room.

II.

Friends, 1991

After Ken Fontenot

We were desperate sex in girls' bodies.
We were girls mothers warned sons about.
We were handcuffed together to a bed at a party.
Sent home together in a cab from a field trip.
We were barns burning for anyone's love.
We were lonely walks to the cemetery & talking to graves.
Blowjobs behind tombstones. Always hoping
to get caught. Always dreaming of escape.
We were talks on the hood of a car. Dreaming
up early dramatic deaths. Scared shitless
of ending up pregnant or poor or fat
or all three. We were learning to drive
a stick shift on gravel roads while eating
ice cream. Flirting for freebies from sweat-
nervous boys at restaurants. We couldn't have
lived any different. We couldn't have saved
one another. We were just trying to survive
the only way we knew how.

There Are No (Simple) Happy Endings

Every fairy tale requires the absence of mother.
Possibly the presence of stepmother. But where
did the mother go? Dead in fever-dream, my dear?
Lips burning prayers to Jesus, your tiny palm
pinning a cool cloth to her forehead?
This is a different story. *The Tale*
of the Mother Who Left.

Every day the same. Putting the food in,
cleaning up what comes out. A child
is a type of worm in its infancy.
But a worm everyone seems to adore.
Strange larva, always wanting more.

And it is this always-wanting-always-touching
that blurs the border between
parasite/predator/predator/prey.
But which escape to plan?

There is the crying-crying-won't-stop-crying
melon-thud of head into wall. Ohmigod, I'm so
sorry, Ohmigod I'm so sorry. But then the stunned
beauty of silence. The calm call to the police.
Waiting in the sun and fresh air of the new world
outside of the screaming—

Or petal bloom of blood
underwater. Crush-metal of car into concrete.
All the mother ever wants is silence. All she
wants to be is alone. To drown in the river
or whisky, to marry the knife or the pills. To free-
fall eight stories, but with or without
the baby?

And this is where we learn
The Mother Who Left is hero/not monster.
To walk away, board the bus, step up
into the cab of the big rig, telling the trucker
Thank you. I've just got to get out of here
is the same story as giving the child love.

When Lights Flash, Bridge Is Up

*two sentences borrowed from the article "The Bridge's Long Shadow" by Jane Seyd

I was in the City of Bridges, always nervous,
always crossing water to get anywhere.
The lane changes needed before the GPS
voice could say them. The Morrison Bridge,
The Hawthorne Bridge, The Burnside
Bridge, The Steel Bridge. Bridges to cross
between the restaurant we'd wanted to go to
and the one that was open. The bridge
we thought we'd turned onto going
the wrong way until we saw the sign
facing us that said, "When Lights Flash,
Bridge is Up," and we knew we were safe.
I read poetry in a friend's house on the crest
of a mountain, the view breathtaking.
Up there, I knew, the world could belong
to me even if I didn't always belong to it.
She'd put a sign in the yard that said,
"Poetry parking this side," and I felt
that this was a world I could exist in.
Earlier on the meditative path of a solace
garden, I thought of the elephants
I'd seen at the zoo. The ones my son
had fallen in love with, the small circle
that had become their lives. But I tried
to appreciate that we were there,
that Liam loved them. That he wanted
two elephants from the gift shop,
Mama and Baby, because now this
was his idea of *elephant.* When you
and I talked it wasn't so much of loss
but of what we had never had. Those parts

we'd been born without. The pain passed
down from pogrom to shtetl to Auschwitz.
The way fury and fear were more real
to us than love. That day you found
a bridge of your own.
You told yourself:
Here you are.
You can decide to slip
a little bit
and you're gone.

Last Night

Since Liam turned two, it has been less
and less. The gradual stretching and thinning
of the thread between us. But tonight, almost
as if he knows, the night before his third birthday,
he wakes to nurse. He nestles close, a little boy,
so different from the baby I held
in the hospital when the nurses would come in
all concern and abruptness, telling me what
I should be doing. Instructions barely registered
through my Percocet haze. He snuggles in,
the Superman emblem on his top cool
against my stomach, and I think about
before he was born, lying in that same spot
on the bed, watching him flip and roll under
my skin. In the dark, he is all sweetness
and softness, silky head of hair,
and small hands grasping. It is only a few
seconds, and he is asleep again. In a few
hours, he will be three. My sweet boy,
grumpy-awake in morning light,
and I will remember sadly the night before
the last time I ever held him so close.

"And they, since they /
Were not the one dead, turned to their affairs"

After Robert Frost's "Out, Out--"

Every creak becomes a swinging rope, the halo of light
cradling him as he hung in the barn's large doorway. The way
her screams felt like they were coming from somewhere else.

She remembers everything about his neck. Putting her nose
into the crook between head and shoulder, breathing him in
the first time. All the times she worried when he would wear

her necklaces, play with neckties. All her fears about that fragile
stem. When he was first learning to sit up, she would put him on
a blanket, watch his head follow her like a flower tracking the sun.

Later, it was sunscreen and aloe, it was learning to tie a tie,
then medals for track and senior keys, straightening his bowtie for prom,
and lastly the purple when the paramedics cut him down—

How do the mothers go on? The ones who still see the ball chased
into the street, who pass the bike helmet on the hook, dust the trophies
on the shelves of bedrooms never, ever entered, except sometimes?

The Bird Wife

Sky thistle, then sapphire, then eggplant—
she watches the waves for driftwood at first light,
fever-dreams of a piece shaped like a sculpture
of the man she lost to the sea years ago.
Fishing for salmon off the Kenai and then
never heard from again. Just a boat
knocking against the wharf. A black dog
howling on shore. She wonders if someday
she will become a seagull crying her losses.
As a girl when the only ocean she had seen
was the endless wheat, she read that albatrosses
were lost sailors' wives following ships
telling the men, *Be safe—Be safe—Be safe!*
There is someone waiting for you at home.

The Scientist Explains Attraction

She runs her fingers over shelves of amber bottles —
Bergamot, Clary Sage, Eucalyptus, Frankincense,
talks of how we used to meet in the darkness
of woods. How the smells of forests and fern
surrounded our meeting, our mating, the mystery
of man and woman. Even today, Fougère, fern-like,
is the base of men's colognes. Oak moss, lavender,
coumarin. Our bodies still speak the language
of plant odors in the limbic system.
The synthetics, we process as poison.
It takes three generations for a scent to become
part of the lexicon of the body; until then
it is an invader, allergen, hormone-disruptor.
She hypothesizes what scents will attract us
in the future—bubblegum, coffee?
Through tests she has discovered that some scents
that arouse us are a molecule away from
the artificial flavor used in banana slushees.
I think of men I've seen sniffing new tires
in the mechanic's shop, my friend who breathed
in deep every time we drove through road
construction, sighing, "I love the smell of tar."
I think of carcinogen as aphrodisiac, the way
sex and cigarette can become associated
and then just as easily, not. I wonder at this
evolution of the body, try to imagine years
from now, what we will become.

Philomela as Farm Wife

Steam rises from the cup of coffee on the kitchen island,
a pink bra swings from the white-painted corner of cabinet door,
jeans pool on the broad walnut boards of the floor.
When did this transformation begin?
Beginnings are all transformations.
Always at the sink doing dishes, always in the kitchen cooking
or cleaning up after cooking, she imagined herself one of the sparrows
stuck in birdlime that she would beg her father to free
when she was a child.
Before she found the pile, their bodies packed
tight like cotton balls, she'd believed him when he said he let them go;
she'd never imagined him capable of cruelty; she'd never imagined
most of the truths of the farm.
When did this transformation begin?
Beginnings are all transformations.
Now, as a bird, she looks in the same window she's spent years
dreaming out of, wonders what rumors will spread to explain
          her disappearance.

A Catalogue of Pain

After "Shoulder" & "Head" by Anne Greenwood

It radiates under the skin like a sunburst,
like spokes stretching from the center of a wheel.
Some days it is all that holds me together.
These uneven breasts. These lopsided hips.
I am a study in imperfection. It is my one
love, my only constant truth.

      ✻

Centuries ago the dreamstate it brings
would mean I was either witch or wise woman.
Mothers would pull daughters close, hiss
warnings not to be like me. But in times
of love-trouble or when
with child and alone, they would knock on my door,
knowing I would know which herbs,
the right words to incant. Now, this gift
is a burden, an inconvenience. An affliction
that happens mostly to women. A punishment
for the stress of working a man's job.
Everyone looks at me impatiently, says,
Go lie down; oh, take an aspirin, will you?

      ✻

Sometimes it is a sand dollar under the skin
and I am certain if I had the courage to slice
my flesh, release its roundness, break its
brittleness between my thumbs and forefingers,
those five white doves would fly away and release
me—the spirit of Jesus Christ who haunts me

for being a woman, less pure, than his mother
Mary. Women's pains always treated
as penance. Childbirth pains—punishment
for Eve's sin, for carnality. A closed throat—
for speaking against God or husband, the intended
God of the household. But I know it
is the Third Eye. My Tenth Gate to the other realm
where I know more than any man. My internal
tilak, which only I see. Invisible sandalwood paste
because it makes me what I am: Creator, Shakti, Lakshmi,
Every Goddess, Every Mother.

How the Dead Return

I.

For years, my boyfriend from college,
heart-crushed by his steering wheel
came to me in dreams. Sometimes he would

be on my balcony, begging me back. Inexplicably
outside my third floor window. Vampire-like,
every seductive movie Dracula ever acted.

Other times, he would walk in, unaware
he had ever died, ask to use the phone
while I was baking cookies. He would ask

where his mother was, his best friend.
I always awoke before I could tell him.
Before I knew if I could.

II.

Once, I crossed to the other side myself.
A reiki master cradled my head in her hands,
and my brain became my whole body.

The part of me in the hotel was the size
of a newborn, and the rest of me—whatever
had traveled—communed with the dead.

My great-grandpa told me, "You're a good girl—
You're a good girl," and I believed him. I played
with the pets I had lost. Gypsy and Ghost. I was

a child again with them. I reveled in kitten pounce
and soft purr. I didn't know what to do when
I woke up sobbing back into my body.

Reality falls away—

Reality falls away — a voice says,
I've been sleeping with your husband
& hangs up. A doctor's mouth shapes

the word *inoperable*. A gunman walks
into a classroom. The world as it was before
no longer exists. & you understand

all the ways of ending the monster
in folklore — Beheading, silver bullet,
stake through the heart — are acts

of mercy. The monster is merely a victim
who didn't know change was coming,
didn't want the bloodlust, was just

an actor being human, which is
always a process of losing humanity,
devolving into something else

altogether with each cell's division,
each full moon's gravity pulling
blood through the capillaries.

The sudden aversion to garlic,
to holy water. The inability to touch
silver, to stand directly in sunlight —

Today we would describe these as triggers.
Something happened, and now I can't —
Something happened, and now I'm

someone else in some other reality.
If you are reading this, please
scatter skeleton flowers on my grave.

My heart is a diner that never closes ...

I.

Look in this ventricle at the waitress,
giving tired smiles and pouring coffee.
She knows her regulars the way a disappointed
mother measures her children against
the children she dreamed of. She wonders
about the man who comes in every few weeks
for pie — each time, a new girl across from him
abuzz with talk about a movie. What is wrong
with him? Why can't he keep them?
And the woman who comes in sometimes,
salt tracks dried down her cheeks from crying.
When will she be all cried out? Bereft of the thirteen
tablespoons trapped in every human body?
She wants to tell the tear-stained woman he isn't
worth it. Instead, she puts down a coffee,
tells her which pies they have that day. Offers
to warm them for her, add a small cup of butter
to pour over the already oozing pecan. The woman
never eats. She's always shaking. The waitress
used to be that woman before she was the waitress
inside the diner of my heart. Look at the busboy
clearing the tables. He has a quick mind and kind
heart but little English. He likes to glide
through the diner unseen. He is the ghost
of empty cups, saucers with swaths of blueberry,
chocolate, whipped cream smeared across them.
The owner of the diner smokes in the office of my
right atrium. He kills himself drag by drag thinking
this isn't the life he planned. Once, he loved
a woman in my left atrium, and he thought

she loved him. But, really, she was a lover of dreams.
The type who would never settle. Head always
in the clouds even though she was firmly lodged
behind my breastbone. He used to sing her
the sweetest songs. Sometimes they would make
my heart catch. Sometimes, they still do.

II.

A bar so desperate for customers
it refuses to hire a bouncer.
The jukebox plays only
the heartbreakingest honkytonk
you ever heard. It howls
like a wolf chained behind the trailer.
When I was a child, I believed
every word of *The Velveteen Rabbit,*
knew if I loved something enough
it would become real, and I've been
trying ever since. A friend once warned me,
You have a heart big enough for anything.
It's true — stray dogs, rhododendrons,
entire mountain skylines. Right now,
the Tantalus Range is expanding
toward my clavicle. Some day
all of the Great Plains will stretch
across my breastplate. Entire galaxies
will fly to the tips of my fingers.
Someday entropy will tame
the cataclysm. Someday, my star
will fall from the sky.

Once

Once, when we were seahorses, you forgot
our mating dance. I clung to the rock—
to the coral — to the reeds, I let myself drift

away. Knew I would never again be heavy
with eggs. I let the current take me where
it took you. I knew one of us would always

be leaving. The other letting go. Next time
I came home to our apartment, empty as Erik
Satie's. A piano. Your black shoes in the southeast

corner of the room. A lone note in the center
of the small table where we shared our meals.
I dropped the bag I was holding. Roadside beets

and potatoes that had fallen from trucks thudded
on our floor. I heard a rat scuttle in a corner.
Just the words — *Run. Don't try to find me* —

and then maybe something that looked like blood,
so I'd listen. What I'm saying is this. I know this is
the way it is. Will always be. Someone is always

a planet, and someone, a star. Some lives are too big
for one lifetime. Listen to the sea. I'm listening—

I Am Not a Narrative for Your Entertainment

The male poet asks, *Why are you single? What's*
the narrative? like I'm a show he's been meaning
to catch up on. The male poet says, *Remember*

the sexy poems you used to write? You're not
writing mommy poems now, are you? I want
to tell him even my mommy poems are too sexy

for him, especially too sexy. I know because
the tongues that have flickered over my C-section
incision have told me. My abdomen, like Zeus's

head, has sprung warriors. And if that's not sexy
then nothing goddamned is. I want to tell him
I'm single because I'm a beautiful disaster.

Not the Little Match Girl but the whole fireworks
factory ablaze. You can watch me burn for miles,
hear about it on the national news. My every move

is a trending topic on Facebook and Twitter.
You just didn't know because you'd been blocked
from my universe.

The Sin Eater

Always the misfit, the outcast. Cast out of the village
when I was twelve, when my parents both died

of the fever. My red hair, mismatched eyes.
One grey. One green. You never knew what

to make of me. Odd boy. *I can feel him looking
through me*, you'd all say. *What if one of his eyes*

sees the future; the other, the past? What if
the dead eye, the grey one, foresees death?

So now, you need me. When someone's died
before last rites, when you don't know if Ma

or Da had remembered every middling sin,
every little white lie, you send someone to knock

on my door. Usually, it's a nervous, breathless
boy like I was when I was sent from the village.

I grab my good hat, my cane, my black dog
Judas follows. And then, the object of our journey —

your loved one laid out, a bowl of ale, a bit
of bread on their chest. I eat my meal, take

your sixpence, roll my wild eyes — a part
of the act I developed ten years in. I say something

soothing. *Your Ma is at peace. Or, The Gates
of Heaven are now opened to your Da.*

I always tuck a bit of bread into my pocket
for the crows. It's just bread. Gives me a chuckle

you pay me to eat your beer and bread. There's
no Heaven, no Hell, other than what we make

for each other —

Is it Human?

Last night, a neo-Nazi tweeted me a picture
of SS officers measuring a man's nose.
Another said, *Just wait 'til January* — *knock, knock,*

*knock. We'll be putting all of you freaks in cages
soon enough.* I thought of naming. How my father's
Holocaust survivor friend and his wife would coo

over my sister. *So blonde. An angel,* they said.
No one would ever know. I was always *the other
one.* The *Why would you name her that name?*

Even then, even sandy-haired and grey-eyed,
I was the dark angel of my family. I thought
of my college boyfriend who dreamt he was

a camp guard. Who dreamt that he made
an exception. That I should feel lucky not to be
too Jewish. I thought of the philosophy of passing —

the discussions in ethics classes. Isn't my moral
responsibility not to hide? Or if I do hide, to help
others? I thought of last night's neo-Nazi who asked,

Is it human? Thought of the Jewish impulse to answer
a question with a question. The way my friends and I
used to joke, *Whaddya mean, 'what do I mean'?*

Today, I had trouble being human. I spent an hour
studying the same bee gathering pollen from the same
dandelion. I watched her fill her pollen sacs, watched

her wipe each antenna clean in her gleaning.
I felt her good fortune at finding a fall flower.
I felt both of us slowing in the face of winter.

The Con Man's Wife

is the first victim after Truth. Patient Zero
of a disease she doesn't know she's spreading.

You've seen the story before — another family
in the same state. Another wife showing up

for the funeral. You wonder, *How could anyone
be so dumb?* Thinking this makes you feel safe.

Once, I believed anything that was said to me.
I believed I was smart and capable and beautiful.

Once, I believed everything that was said to me.
I believed I was stupid and crazy and dangerous.

Some days I believe I've broken my brain by
believing all this at once. Once, I wanted to be

the last thing you'd want to throw on a gas fire.
Then, I wanted to be the first. Now, I am learning

to be the fire itself. Discovering the lie was like
realizing the salt shaker had been filled with ground

glass all along. You start examining all the places
you've been cut. Picture your stomach shredding

itself like a meat slicer. Then, you think of all
your dinner parties, family meals — all the salt

sprinkled across other plates, all the shakers
passed across the table in pairs. Your stomach

churns now, hungry for its own blood. I spent
six years mourning a boy who didn't die

because he never existed. He was a brilliantly
executed lie, a story fabricated from nothing.

I still send money to the country
he was never born in.

Playing Dolls

Imagine a girl who doesn't know she's real. Imagine Ginger
the makeup artist painting her face backstage saying,
Doing your makeup is like painting a doll.

Look at these eyebrows, these cheekbones, these lashes.
Imagine, *these* — not *yours.*

Suddenly, the girl is a catalogue, a naming of parts.
Maybe she was never a girl to begin with. Imagine Coppélia,
the fabulous doll, dancing the mazurka. Knee, knee, heel, step,

clap, clap. Knee, knee, heel, step, clap, clap. Imagine
being the tin soldier who fires the stage cannon
at the Mouse King. The one who stands still and greets children

after matinee performances. Imagine hearing children ask parents
if you are real. Imagine not knowing.

                    Imagine being under the same type of spell
as the doll who wants to be real. Imagine a man listing parts
the same way — *these tits, this ass, this pussy.* Imagine never belonging

to your own body. Your own body never belonging to you. Imagine
you were programmed only to say *yes* when a man pulls the string.
Imagine when you say *no,* it's like men can't hear it. Like you

are just a doll who says *yes* and *Momma* and *sleepy.* Like when
they lay you down, your eyes close, and you don't remember
anything that happens next. Imagine the world that tells you
        this is your fault.

Not Dr. Coppélius or Drosselmeyer or Balanchine. You are the one
who has starved yourself to the thinness of a slip, never taught yourself
to speak using your wooden tongue. You are the one who had to cut

the strings that were visible only to you. Stare down
the hammer above your porcelain skull. You know your body
is misshapen from following the choreographer's uneven directions.
Now, what are you going to do to fix it?

III.

Thirteen Ways of Looking at a Pelican

I.

The lone pelican in the reeds
of river's edge seemed odd.
I stopped — watched —
did nothing.

Later in the paper the story
of its broken wing,
likely caused
by flying into a wire.

That it would probably be
euthanized. *When you see
a pelican alone, it usually
means something is wrong,*
said the wildlife expert.

My self-doubt that kept me
from calling. Did I cause that pelican
more hours of suffering
or gift it a few more hours
of floating in the reeds,
a little while longer to bob
in the gentle current,
the coolness of water over webbed feet?

Forgive me, pelican. I also, am always alone,
also fly too recklessly for my own good.

2.

When I told you about the pelican —
that I thought I should have called someone.
You said, *That's your problem. You always
doubt your instincts.*
As a woman, I've been taught to ignore
connections. The ones between myself
and the moon, the tides
internal and external.
The way the pelican and I
for an instant
were one.

3.

The pelicans sit on the rocks preening,
a section of concert violinists bowing

apricot bills against snow velvet down
of breast. I wonder if they can hear

the friction of their surfaces one against
the other. If there is a making of music

out of their bodies. I remember them
later when the photographer says,

When you touch yourself,
when your fingers skim

the hollow between throat and clavicle
you are telling the viewer, Oh, my skin

is so soft, don't you wish you could
touch it?

4.

The young man and his friends float the river
the Fourth of July
                              Downstream are parade
sounds   neighing of horses   marching bands
salvos of gunfire

Here, there is only the river   soft lap of water
against the inner tube

                        The peace only occasionally
interrupted by an *Oh shit!* when a raft scuffs a rock
gets hung up on a branch

            Miraculously, the pelicans sit still on the rocks
inspecting from ice blue eyes on either side of long beaks

                    Their heads tilt this way and that
but otherwise they are unmoved by these creatures

the only ones larger than they who float downstream
            The young man has the odd feeling he has never
been so close to another breathing thing

He looks into the ice blue of the pelican's eye as he floats
            by   thinks of the day his eye drew this much
                        attention   Hiding under the bill of his cap

eye surrounded by magenta bruise, fidgeting to the rhythm
of fluorescent light flicker   the professor asking

My God, what happened?

He recalls the feel of the lie slipping out of his mouth

A baseball I didn't catch

5.

We come home with the groceries, and I see
the slow V of pelicans floating over the neighborhood,
try to tell if they are tracing the river.

I've heard they are one of the few bird species
that fly "for fun." I wonder what that means,
try to imagine what it must feel like

to soar on thermals for up to fifteen miles
without flapping a wing, to climb the pillows
of hot air, drop down into coolness

to gain speed. This is called *dynamic soaring.*
I didn't used to be so fascinated by anything
but now, I pull out my phone, try to record them.

They are immortalized as radar blips over
my neighbors' chimney; in the background
my dog barks, my son is excited to be allowed

to run to the porch by himself. How could anything
be so effortless? I wonder what I might miss
if I were afforded their abilities, their innate sense

of measuring air temperature through their nostrils,
of spotting a single fish from sixty feet above water —
All I can imagine missing is the grey house

with its hot pink door I drive by every day.

6.

With the camera strapped to his bill,
we peer into his blinking eyes;

he looks like any awkward son
unsure of what he is doing.

Lake Tanganyika, the Mahale Mountains
spread in the distance.

Baobab's "Music for a Movie" crescendos
as the bird glides over water.

His first flight recorded,
become a GoPro commercial

with over 3,000,000 YouTube views,
he is a media sensation.

Since being blown in on the storm,
Big Bird lives a charmed life,

at the $1,000 per person, per night resort.
But what does the orphaned

pelican make of the humans
who taught him to fly by running the beach,

flapping their arms? Does he wonder why
they never leave the ground? Does he know

he is a metaphor for loneliness?

7.

But what is the river without the pelicans?
It is still the herons stalking minnows in the reeds
and the two trees where their twelve nests rest
beyond the picnic pavilion.

It is the osprey hovering above the river
and the Pacific Power linemen who built
the new nesting platform while the osprey
wintered in South America.

It is the wood ducks and mallards, the flit
and *seeeee-yeeee* song of red-winged blackbird.
The slate arrows of doves that throw themselves
down to river's edge after seeds.

It is otter and mink, the deer that come down
from the ridge, the cattle from open range
who amble down mountain on hot days.
It is Coho and Chinook, steelhead
and salmon. The train tracks which follow

the river from Gibbon to river mouth. Where
one night, a boy lay his head, and later
in the high school gym, I hugged his mother,
and said, *I'm so sorry about your son.*

The river is every single body
that has been pulled out of it, the ghosts
that walk the levee. But today, there were
pelicans, two breeding pairs, so we move on.

8.

We must remind ourselves
the pelican is an opportunist.
Do not be surprised when
it snatches a duckling,
flings it up so it
drops in headfirst,
takes water into its bill,
so the duckling
will drown
in its gullet.
We have trouble accepting
when nature goes against
what we see as order.
Cannibalism, for instance,
or an insect eating
a mouse. We act horrified
because we like to forget
that we are exactly
the same.

9.

I want to give Liam a love
of language, of nature. He is just beginning
to differentiate birds. So far, there is generic
boo-id. And *owww-ell.* Anything the size
of a duck is a *dutch.* A peacock is an *up-cock.*
We try not to laugh, don't want to make
him self-conscious even though *shirt*
and *shorts* and *socks* all sound obscene.
When we walk along the levee
the pelicans are *dutch.* I try to correct
him until I realize their shape classification
is listed as "ducklike"; sometimes, already,
he is more observant than I am. Like the day
we were walking and I heard him say,
Sssssss, and thought he was playing,
then, thought he had found a toy snake,
until I reached down to touch it,
saw the warm flick of the tongue.
Little striped whipsnake, trying
to make his way to the river.
I attempted to lift him with a stick
while Liam hissed excitedly, *Sssss!*
Sssss! and then, along came a boy
on a skateboard, who stopped,
lifted him over the side of the levee
bare-handed, dropped him into
the rocks to slither to water.
I want my son to be like that brave boy
so gentle and unafraid all at once.

10.

The hamerkop and shoebill bridge pelican and stork,
sometimes listed in one order, sometimes shifted
to the other.

Hamerkop = Ciconiiformes or Pelecaniformes?
Shoebill = Ciconiiformes or Pelecaniformes?

In Ancient Greek *Pelekan* < *Pelekys* = *axe,*
that great bill its distinguishing feature,
but confusingly, woodpecker was *Pelekys* as well.

In proto-German the stork is *sturkaz* = *stark,*
but we do not know if this describes his whiteness
or his stiff manner.

daboro = *bringer of wealth or bringer of life* as in the myth that storks deliver ba-
bies

Or in Estonian *toonekurg* = *crane of the underworld,* in the case
of the black stork, because the black stork is the bringer of death.

Uda-faro = *walker of swamps* can be either.

With their wide, white wingspans, fringe of coal black flight feathers;
other than outstretch of legs and neck, they are identical from below.

In Egypt, *ba,* the soul of a person was symbolized as
A stork at one's death meant maybe the beloved
        could be brought back to life.

Henet, pelican goddess, mother of the king, perhaps mother
of all of Egypt, afforded safe passage to the afterlife.

This was a different type of hope. The open mouth of the pelican sym-
bolized the opening of tomb to the next world where the beloved would
wait for you.

Stork : pelican : : rebirth : afterlife.

II.

For centuries it was believed that the pelican
was an allegory for Christ. That the young
would begin with their new, sharp beaks,

to wound their parents, drawing their blood,
and the parents, in their anger, would smite them.
After three days of mourning the mother (some

accounts say the father) would open its breast,
and the hot drops of blood would bring the young
back to life. This allegory was to teach of Christ's

love. His sacrifice on the cross. Bartholomaeus
Anglicus wrote in the 13th Century, *The pelican
loveth too much her children.* The same way

I was taught that Adam's sin was uxoriousness.
But I was taught that we could never love Christ
too much, that we were to devote our lives to Him.

Instead, I choose the mountains, the rivers.
They open their hearts to us every day
no matter how we wound them.

12.

Booth points out his favorite graffiti
in my town, and I'm amazed I've never
noticed after living here eight years,
under the Main Street Bridge, someone
has spray-painted, *Angela, I love you.*
Fix me. It's always these moments
of public brokenness that undo me.
Like that pelican with the shattered ulna
floating alone on the river, until his rescue
which ended in being put to sleep.
The way the stages of his extrication
played out in pictures, but until the end
of the article you didn't realize by the time
you'd read it, he was already dead.
Yesterday, there were four pelicans;
today, three. I wonder when one leaves
the flock how they feel, if they tell
themselves they'll soon be flying after —

13.

Ecologists in Australia look to the pelican for clues
on water conservation. After all, the pelican

has survived on the driest continent for 30 million years.
They are trying to determine if pelicans know

when rains are coming or if they watch the formation
of rivers through flash flooding, following water

to the newly formed basin lake, flying 400 miles per day.
Perhaps they have a sense we don't, a sort of flood memory,

because the Lake Eyre pelicans breed only when it rains,
sometimes waiting a decade or more between seasons.

Here, on the Columbia, on the Umatilla, we are just starting
to watch the pelican. There have been 17,000 brown pelicans

on East Sand Island, an increase in the numbers of white pelicans
on the Umatilla. Will they keep traveling north as our planet warms?

What will become of all of us, if we don't listen?

The video referenced in section 6 can be found at:
http://www.youtube.com/watch?v=_YEyzvtMx3s

IV.

Prayer to the God of Small Things

I've been too much for the solitary world,
always spilling out at the seams. The woman
who can't keep one life, one husband, one state —

If only you could make yourself less. Be quieter.
Hold something back. Maybe be less nice.
You could be an Ice Queen — if you'd just
turn down the heat.

      I refuse to lose at the game
they've made me play, but today, just once, I'll pray
to the God of Small Things. Ask to be Queen
of the Republic of the Freckle Next to Your Right Eye.

I know you'll never be mine; we aren't wired that way,
but I want to claim this sacred spot no matter
what other women or men or continents claim

the rest of you. Please let me dwell
in the smallness of this speck that disappears
when you smile. Let me weather the winds
fanned by your eyelashes.

I'll be a magnanimous
queen. I'll give anything if the God of Small Things
will let me in.

First Flight

For my son, who confused "airplanes" and "babies"

When the baby learned to fly, he flew
over wind-tree and grass-green. Neigh-
horse and moo-cow. He stopped
over the river like an osprey
looking for swish-fish. The wind
through the canyon tickled his tree-
toes. He learned to nap
in the willow's branches like
a sleepy snake. At night, he would
feel the pull of the sinking sun
and fly for his mother-nest. *Home.*

Private Property

for Andrew Stancek

The poet says, *This is for you; buy something warm,*
presses enough cash into the homeless man's small palm
that I wonder if he knows what he's holding,

if it's enough to put him in danger. The homeless man
keeps going through the trash outside the fancy restaurant
we're leaving. The one where I'll be paying off my meal

for months. He puts a Gatorade bottle, a Rockstar can
into his shopping cart. The policeman says, *You can't do that.*
The homeless man darts down the street the way I used

to watch roaches scatter when I'd turn on the kitchen lights
in Texas. *Why? Why can't he do that?* the poet asks,
his central European accent thick, emotion making his

English stick in his mouth. *The trash here is private property,*
the cop says. His job, to keep the homeless out of sight, away
from the glitzy lights of *L.A. Live.* I want to tell the poet

that what he did was lovely, right. But my voice is a trapped
animal that can't crawl out my throat. The poet folds his long
body into the cab, where we all feel him quake with quiet rage.

Curious George Loves the Man with the Yellow Hat

But is this really love, or because the man looks
like a banana? The way I would find my beige
Camry covered with iridescent champagne

dragonflies every spring. The same way I fell
for a cowboy with a Johnny Cash voice
and a black hat. Or an Indian straight out

of an in-love-with-a-white-teacher Harlequin
plot. Instead of laying me on deerskins in front
of a fire, there were Pendleton blankets chorused

by radiator clicks and clangs. How much of love
is love? How much the geometry of jawline
and hip ratio, search for the golden spiral?

An imagined instance of lullaby from milk-
sleep and breast-cradle? How much the softness
of skin against skin? In my mind I know

I shouldn't love you, but it's my heart
that always wins.

The Old Woman in the Forest

"You've saved me and set me free
from the power of the old woman," he said.
—*Grimm's Fairy Tales*

Don't believe princes. Sometimes, they're not even princes.
He might be a robber who killed the royal family and dressed
in their finery. A swineherd who taught himself to read

by the light of the fire. Even a woodsman sent
to cut out the heart of your own cousin. The reason
you'll believe the words that fall from his lips

is you want to believe that he is your future. I am
your future, and that is your biggest fear. You don't
want to look in a mirror and see this lined face,

this softened body, but the truth is, I was just like you —
did all the things you do —Took a basket to my ailing
grandma in the wood, pricked my finger on a spindle

when I tried my hand at spinning straw into gold.
I even once danced at a ball and lost a shoe like
the lame horse I was. I am your future.

Some frogs are just frogs. Some trees are just trees.
Heed me, my child, don't trust men who claim
to be princes, who claim to possess golden keys.

*The tale this poem is based on can be found at
http://www.pitt.edu/~dash/grimm123.html

Finding Place

I always watched as my grandfather opened the needle.
Sometimes he offered to let me push its point under

his skin, but I never said yes. My sister was always the brave one.
But now when I wonder about her, I'm not sure how this works.

How many years has it been since she has left the basement,
the house? She was the one who rode my friends' horses.

I was always the coward, the most useless girl on a farm.
Unable to dock puppies' tails, give injections, butchering

wasn't even an option. The first time I swore, I was pilling
a calf, but I could never do anything that would break the skin.

Even cranking the meat grinder was too much, knowing that
I might once have loved what was being reduced to fibers

of muscle. When that calf died, I asked where we would bury it,
and when my uncle and grandpa laughed, said it would go

to the fertilizer plant, something in me broke. But I'll always love
a farm. I am the goddess of bicycle rides to waterlily covered lakes.

Lover of every wildflower in the field. I'll give up anything
to capture a ray of sunlight shining through the Queen Anne's lace.

When I Was Bluebeard's Wife

I didn't fear the murder room, didn't loathe the bristle
of blue whiskers on my neck, my breasts. I didn't even
flinch at the knife. I feared his finding a wife who

would be his equal. Her azure hair, her lily skin.
The love they would make. I practiced first cutting
on myself — my white thighs. Willed the servant girl

to hold the mirror so I could draw a knife across
my buttock. The blood was quite beautiful;
it looked like berry-stain I remembered from when

I was a girl. But when I held kittens, rabbits, piglets,
I knew I could never make the cut on someone other
than myself. He would find a girl to marry who was

not quite human. A selkie, a changeling. He would
make her a gold key to wear on a chain hidden
between her breasts. She would be able to slice

anyone's throat while still smiling, looking them
in the eyes. She would be the one to put my head

on the wall.

This Old House

I.

This is the moose "Welcome to Our Home" sign he bought
garage-saling because addicts just trade in their addictions
for new ones. Heroin for yard-saling for Mountain Dew.

This is the kitchen where he called me "Sarah" for Sarah
Palin making the elk chili just right. The kitchen where
I made the pie he said wasn't a real pie because the middle

wasn't moist enough, where I processed more apples
than I weigh while he slept though we both worked all year
tending the trees because I could do all the work, but

he couldn't do "women's work," or what was the point
of having a wife? This is the kitchen where another he
ripped out a wall, tore up a floor, erased all evidence of

the other man. Never finished. Left a sign that announced
the kitchen was his, diner style in bright chalk. This is
the dishwasher I couldn't load right because I'm fucking

retarded because no one ever taught me a fucking thing,
and he was just trying to teach, but I never listened.
I'm fucking useless at home and should go back to the office

where I'm good for something. This is the bathroom where
I spent too much time getting ready. Where I looked in
the full-length mirror before he asked, "Is that what

you're wearing?" every day. Some days he was just
kidding. Some days the browns didn't match. This is
where another he ripped out a wall. Didn't finish it.

Where I got yelled at for not caulking the grab bars.
Where I could have let poison mold grow through
the whole house. Was I fucking stupid? Didn't I know

how to take care of things? These were simple repairs
I should be able to take care of myself. This is the room
where my female body was so disgusting, he had to buy

a new trash can because I should be ashamed of
my periods. Hide all the secrets of my body even
from him. This is where he was showering when

I asked why there were all these messages from her
on his phone. This is the cabinet where I kept the pills
to keep from getting pregnant and the pills to get pregnant

and the pills to make me the best incubator and the pills
to keep me the quietest puppet. To make me unable to feel
the blowups, the nothings, the death by a thousand cuts

every day.

II.

And this is the bedroom —
the bedroom
the bedroom —
where sometimes I was so sexy
and sometimes I was a good girl
and a dumb bitch and a stupid cunt.
And once there was a he who fucked me
ten times a day — and this was control
and once one who wanted me once a year
and this was control. This is a new doorknob
because once I locked the door
        just to stop the yelling,
        and he pulled it off.
        You might want to know
which he was which. That isn't the point.
What I'm trying to say is that there were
ten years
I wasn't in my own body.
Things happened
in this house that
I don't know how
to write.

III. (*Things that I threw away*)

The curtains because I have nothing to hide.
The curtains because while I was decorating
for Christmas he was having an affair.
The curtains because when the sun shone through
the red ones all I could see was Othello suffocating
Desdemona in the red silk sheets of their marriage bed.

Any of the underwear he ever liked. Any of the underwear
he might have touched. Underwear, because he asked
the other woman what kind of underwear a super mom wears.

Our wedding rings, I tied with twine
to an art installation on memory
while my students watched.

The pie pans, the loaf pans, the apple mill.
And lastly, my heart, my heart, my heart —

IV. (This Summer)

My son and I color in bed, and he tells me, "You're a princess,
and I'm a knight." He says that he'll rescue me.

"What if I'm a princess and a knight?" He tries drawing
a princess with a sword. He asks, "What about dragons?"

"What if the princess *is* the dragon?" I ask him. "What if she's
the fire?" We go outside. Take breakfast to the porch. See how

close to not-human we can be. See how close the finches
come to landing on us. Even today I was still enough that I could

feel the vibration of a hummingbird's wings on my cheek. It felt
like a million blinking eyelashes. We listen to the sparrows

disassemble the house. If we go into the garage, they are riotous.
The attic I had to squeeze into to reset the garage door is filled

with their clamor. They could fly the garage away at any second.
This is my summer of climbing high enough to see two states

at once, of dreaming what animal I'll be in my next incarnation,
of the deer and me studying each other as sisters. This is the summer

of wildfires disappearing houses in every direction —
and I'm not even afraid.

V. (The Porch)

I am learning the language of starlings and doves,
of house sparrows, and finches. Each species has
a favorite seed. Favorite type of feeder. The doves

move from telephone pole to tree, occasionally
to porch. Are the most wary of me. Starlings,
the next. Speckled bodies drift down to peck suet

from metal cages chained to the fence.
When I am in the house, they flood the yard,
twenty to forty at a time. Disappear when I enter

their world. The sparrows treat me like a servant
who lives in another part of their home. Line the roof
until I fill the feeder. Chirp so loud the cheap aluminum

gutters vibrate until they are satisfied. Finches
send a scout to see what I am doing. If the ladder
is out, if the feeders are filled, if I have turned on

the spigot. Until everything is to their liking,
the scout flies at me over and over. Little brave one,
looking out for his flock. I sit amidst the ruin

and watch their lives. Next to me, the chairs I repainted
after he left them in the yard to rot. The hole burned
into the deck by the meat smoker he left unattended.

Each day, the same. Coffee on the porch in the morning. Beer on the porch at dusk. Cue the hummingbird. Cue the yellow swallowtail. This is the only certainty I need.

VI.

It's tempting to start over — a brand new life. There is a cabin
just off a hiking trail I'm in love with. I could take wildlife photos,
collect pine sap for my friend the herbalist. Still, it's nothing

that will enable me to make a living. The house for sale
around the block is too expensive, is next to the woman
my second husband had an affair with. At what point

isn't everything triggering? At what point might my life
be mine again? There are experts who help you throw away
everything connected with abuse — this sexy, one-shouldered

top, the rib brace hiding on the floor of my closet. But
at what point isn't that everything? When do you decide
not to throw yourself away, too?

                                   Leaving this house
after ten years would feel like letting them win —
my second husband, my son's father. I love the sloped

A-line of the cottage front, the steep roof that sloughs
off the snow. I've filled out loan papers, looked at paint
colors — *fun yellow, denim.* Why does everything cost

so much money? Why do men always get to leave everything
behind and start over? Most days, I know that I'm wreckage,
debris. This is my summer of learning what it's like to live

outside of survival mode. Still, there's so much I don't understand —
arranging things, decorating. I feel like those Holocaust survivors
who asked their children, *Well, you aren't a lampshade, are you?*

whenever they would complain about something trivial. I've
never thought about cabinets and countertops. Only how not
to be beaten, how not to be killed. I used to think, *Fuck you,*

when my friends showed me paint swatches, their new bedding.
I didn't even understand the point. Thinking about these things
still seems silly, but this is my house, and I want to fix it.

Besides, if I leave, how will my little birds find me?

Left and Leaving, 2016

The crow that I wrapped in a shawl and drove to the sanctuary.
I had hoped it was just a broken wing, that they could set it.

When they told me that he had been shot, that there was still
a bullet lodged in his body, I tried to be thankful for feeling

what life was left as he scratched the side of the box
I had placed him in for the drive. The disabled puppy

that would never walk that we tried to save at the shelter.
I touched my nose to her nose when she was held up to me.

Breathed in her puppy breath. I wanted her to feel like
she was surrounded by mothers even though her own

had refused to feed her. Had chosen, instead, to keep the rest
of the litter alive. The maimed kitten a man brought in

to be euthanized. I gave him the forms for emergency assistance,
left the room while he filled them out. My own cat I held, forehead

to forehead, whispering, "You've been the best cat ever. I love you,
I love you, I love you," until his body went limp. My best friend

whose summer has been telling her daughters goodbye, making
video letters of the advice she'll give them each year, after she's gone.

All this, and the lover who is moving to another continent,
who keeps saying he doesn't want to hurt me. I want him to know

that that's what love is — an inevitable entropy toward pain.
No matter the beginning or the middle, it is all a building

toward leaving. There is no happily ever after — the fairy tales
are lies. We only each have what we were able to cling to.

After Mary Oliver

"Someone I loved once gave me a box full of darkness.
It took me years to understand that this, too, was a gift."
——Mary Oliver

I have become a lover of solitude.
Feeder of finches, savior of starlings
and sparrows. After you, I no longer
want to be human. I will be woodsprite.
River imp. I might believe in love
when I become a river otter, a dove.
All of the pressure of human relationships
is too much. It has been the one fantastic
failure of my life. The one puzzle piece
I've never been able to make fit.
Once, after a poetry reading, a past life
regressionist said to me, "We need
to find out what makes you attract
this type of man." I didn't go because
I'm rebuilding myself very deliberately.
I would have wanted her to tell me that
I'm still not fully human — that that's why
I haven't figured human love out.
That there's been a terrible mistake.
That it will never have to happen again.

Shaindel Beers is the author of three full-length poetry collections, *A Brief History of Time* (2009), *The Children's War and Other Poems* (2013), both from Salt Publishing, and *Secure Your Own Mask* (2018), from White Pine Press. She teaches at Blue Mountain Community College in Pendleton, Oregon, where she lives with her son Liam, and serves as Poetry Editor of *Contrary Magazine*.

ACKNOWLEDGMENTS *(continued from copyright page)*

Tupelo Quarterly: "Unfriending the Dead."
Contrappasso Magazine: "3.22 Miles," "After *Milkpour* #5 by Jessica Plattner," and "Friends, 1991."
Poetry South: "The Secret Rabbit" and "Once."
Suisin Valley Review: "The Interview."
Visual Verse: "Perspective."
IthacaLit: "There Are No (Simple) Happy Endings."
Medical Journal of Australia: "When Lights Flash, Bridge Is Up" and "Is it Human?"
Tahoma Literary Review: "And they, since they / Were not the one dead, turned to their affairs."
Colloquium: "The Bird Wife" and "Philomela as Farm Wife."
TAB: The Journal of Poetry and Poetics: "A Catalogue of Pain" (in excerpt).
Undead: A Poetry Anthology of Ghouls, Ghosts, and More!: "How the Dead Return."
Queen of Cups: "Reality falls away—," "I Am Not a Narrative for Your Entertainment," and "Prayer to the God of Small Things."
Poetry City, USA: "My heart is a diner that never closes ..." (Part I) and "The Con Man's Wife."
Tinderbox Poetry Journal: "My heart is a diner that never closes ..." (Part II) and "Curious George Loves the Man with the Yellow Hat."
Columbia Poetry Review: "Once."
Cascadia Review: "Thirteen Ways of Looking at a Pelican."
Hyperlexia: "Part 9 from Thirteen Ways of Looking at a Pelican."
The Poet's Quest for God: "Thirteen Ways of Looking at a Pelican" (Part II).
Hapax: "First Flight."
Chantarelle's Notebook: "Private Property" and "This Old House."
Prime Number Magazine: "When I Was Bluebeard's Wife."

"The Mechatronic Bird Falls in Love with the Real and Vice Versa" is a musical collaboration with Skip vonKuske available on SoundCloud.

"When we were knife throwers" and "Self-Portrait as Rosinback Rider" are musical collaborations with Jesse Ahmann available on YouTube.

THE WHITE PINE PRESS POETRY PRIZE

Vol. 23: *Secure Your Own Mask* by Shaindel Beers. Selected by Alan Michael Parker.

Vol. 22: *Bread From a Stranger's Oven* by Janlori Goldman. Selected by Laure-Anne Bosselaar.

Vol. 21: *The Brighter House* by Kim Garcia. Selected by Jericho Brown.

Vol. 20: *Some Girls* by Janet McNally. Selected by Ellen Bass.

Vol. 19: *Risk* by Tim Skeen. Selected by Gary Young.

Vol. 18: *What Euclid's Third Axiom Neglects to Mention About Circles* by Carolyn Moore. Selected by Patricia Spears Jones.

Vol. 17: *Notes from the Journey Westward* by Joe Wilkins. Selected by Samuel Green.

Vol. 16: *Still Life* by Alexander Long. Selected by Aliki Barnstone.

Vol. 15: *Letters From the Emily Dickinson Room* by Kelli Russell Agodon. Selected by Carl Dennis.

Vol. 14: *In Advance of All Parting* by Ansie Baird. Selected by Roo Borson.

Vol. 13: *Ghost Alphabet* by Al Maginnes. Selected by Peter Johnson.

Vol. 12: *Paper Pavilion* by Jennifer Kwon Dobbs. Selected by Genie Zeiger.

Vol. 11: *The Trouble with a Short Horse in Montana* by Roy Bentley. Selected by John Brandi.

Vol. 10: *The Precarious Rhetoric of Angels* by George Looney. Selected by Nin Andrews.

Vol. 9: *The Burning Point* by Frances Richey. Selected by Stephen Corey.

Vol. 8: *Watching Cartoons Before Attending A Funeral* by John Surowiecki. Selected by C.D. Wright.

Vol. 7: *My Father Sings, To My Embarrassment* by Sandra Castillo. Selected by Cornelius Eady.

Vol. 6: *If Not For These Wrinkles of Darkness* by Stephen Frech. Selected by Pattiann Rogers.

Vol. 5: *Trouble in History* by David Keller. Selected by Pablo Medina.

Vol. 4: *Winged Insects* by Joel Long. Selected by Jane Hirshfield.

Vol. 3: *A Gathering of Mother Tongues* by Jacqueline Joan Johnson. Selected by Maurice Kenny.

Vol. 2: *Bodily Course* by Deborah Gorlin. Selected by Mekeel McBride.

Vol. 1: *Zoo & Cathedral* by Nancy Johnson. Selected by David St. John.